The PONY EXPRESS

LAUREL VAN DER LINDE

A TIMESTOP BOOK

New York

Maxwell Macmillan Canada
Toronto

Maxwell Macmillan International
New York   Oxford   Singapore   Sydney

For Gower

On the cover: The departure of the first Pony Express rider from Pike's Peak stables in St. Joseph, Missouri on April 3, 1860. (Courtesy of the St. Joseph Museum.)
Book design: Deborah Fillion
Map on pages 32–33 drawn by Kathie Kelleher

New Discovery Books
Macmillan Publishing Company
866 Third Avenue
New York, NY 10022

Maxwell Macmillan Canada, Inc.
1200 Eglinton Avenue East
Suite 200
Don Mills, Ontario M3C 3N1

Macmillan Publishing Company is part of the Maxwell Communication Group of Companies

First edition
Printed in the United States of America
10 9 8 7 6 5 4 3 2 1

Library of Congress Cataloging-in-Publication Data
Van der Linde, Laurel, 1952-
    The pony express / by Laurel van der Linde.
       p.   cm.
    "A Timestop Book."
    Includes bibliographical references and index.
    Summary: Surveys the history of the Pony Express, from its creation at the time of the Gold Rush to its demise at the start of the Civil War. Includes profiles of famous riders.
    ISBN 0-02-759056-9
    1. Pony express—History—Juvenile literature. 2. Postal service—United States—History—Juvenile Literature. [1. Pony express. 2. West (U.S.)—History.]   I. Title.
HE6375.P65V36   1993
383'.143'0973—dc20   92-31756

Contents

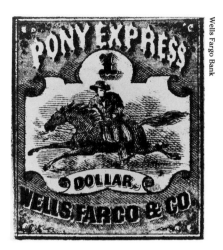

Pony Express postage stamp

INTRODUCTION

✪

Hoofbeats across America

✪

Night was fast approaching as Bob Haslam spurred his pony into the Nevada desert sage. The brush was high—high enough for Indians to hide in. As Bob headed west, he could not erase the gruesome picture of Cold Spring Station from his mind—the stock driven off by Indians, the stationmaster murdered.

Since there had been no change of horses for him at the Pony Express relay station, Bob had no choice but to ask his animal to do double duty. He let his horse drink and then pressed on. He had to get the mail to Sand Springs. He had to warn the people there—if the Indians hadn't already made their presence known.

The lonely howl of a coyote pierced the still, spring air of 1860, sending chills up Bob's spine. He could feel his pony's heart pounding—in both anticipation and fear. The pony pricked its ears, twitching them

*Pony Bob carrying the news of Abraham Lincoln's election
to a Pony Express Telegraph Station*

forward, sideways, backward. Bob studied those ears. If they remained pointed in one direction or lay flat, it was a sure sign of Indians lying in the sage waiting to ambush.

Bob dropped the reins and asked the exhausted animal to give him more speed. He knew his life and the lives of those waiting at Sand Springs depended on this hardy little fellow. Bob and his pony continued at a steady gallop. He could feel the sides of the pony's ribs heaving against his boots. The brush scratched against Bob's legs as he urged the pony forward.

Bob's mind raced back over the events of the past few hours. Yesterday afternoon he had left his home station, Friday's, for his normally scheduled run east. When he arrived at Reed's Relay Station, he found the place deserted and no fresh horse waiting for him. All the men and horses had gone to fight the Pah-Ute Indians who had burned Williams' Station and killed five of its men two days earlier. Bob fed his horse at Reed's and pressed on to the next relay station.

Thundering into Buckland's Station, Bob expected to find his relief rider, Johnson Richardson, ready to take over as scheduled. But Richardson was scared. He had heard of the Indian uprising and flatly refused to ride his route through "Pah-Ute Hell."

Despite the fact that he had already ridden 75 miles (121 kilometers), 19-year-old Bob Haslam felt it was his duty to continue. The company motto, "The mail must go through," had been thoroughly drummed into Bob Haslam by his employers. Buckland's stationmaster, W. C. Marley, offered him a $50 bonus if he would continue the run. Well, they didn't call him "Pony" Bob for nothing. Besides, the Pony Express had been in operation only two months. It could not fail now.

Bob mounted a fresh horse and pounded on to Sand Springs, then Cold Spring, where he discovered the massacred body of the stationmaster. When he finally arrived at Smith's Creek Station, he had put 190 miles (306 kilometers) behind his ponies' hooves, more than double his scheduled route. At Smith's Creek, Jay G. Kelley relieved Haslam of his duties and continued the mail on its eastward run.

But Bob's adventure was far from over. Eight hours later, he took the westbound mail and started back to Cold Spring. Again, he watered his horse in the shadow of the stationmaster's corpse and pressed on.

Bob's pony was lathered in sweat now, steam rising from its shoulders and flanks in the cool night air. They were almost at Sand Springs now. Would it still be there? Or would it be burned to the ground like Williams' Station?

The moon rose in the May sky. Bob strained his eyes to see. He could just make out the outline of the adobe building that was Sand Springs Station. But would anyone still be left alive? Bob soon discovered that only the stock tender had remained at Sand Springs. The other men had gone to fight the Indians. Bob told him about the raid on Cold Spring

Station, and the stock tender quickly agreed to continue on with Bob to Carson Sink. Later, they would learn that Sand Springs was attacked by Indians the following morning.

There were 15 men at Carson Sink. They were armed and ready to fight the Indians. Bob rested an hour and then, after dark, pressed on to Buckland's Station alone. He was running three and a half hours behind schedule when he arrived at Buckland's—not bad, considering all the upheaval and lack of fresh horses.

Stationmaster Marley was so happy to see Bob still alive that he offered to double his bonus if Bob would finish the run to Friday's Station. Keyed up from all the excitement, Bob was more than ready to ride up into the Sierra Nevada and back to Friday's, his home station, nestled at the foot of the mountains near Lake Tahoe. He had ridden 380 miles (612 kilometers) in 36 hours—the longest ride in the short history of the Pony Express.

It is tales such as this one about "Pony" Bob Haslam that turn the story of the Pony Express into the stuff of legend. The Pony Express, often called simply the Pony, also had far-reaching effects. From April 1860 to October 1861, the hoofbeats of the Pony were heard not only in the American wilderness, but around the world. Thundering across the nearly 2,000-mile (3,200-kilometer) stretch between St. Joseph, Missouri, in the east and Sacramento, California, in the west, the Pony Express was the model of efficiency, dedication, and good old American know-how.

But if its work was so well done, why did it have such a short life? And if this mail service across the continent was so important to the U.S. government, why was it run by a private business rather than the U.S. Post Office? The high costs of running the Pony Express fell to the well-known freighting firm of Russell, Majors, and Waddell. So difficult was the work that only the best horses, the most fearless riders, and the toughest, most determined men were hired. At a salary of $25 a week, their price was high compared to other wages of that time. But their loyalty to the work could be depended on in a crisis.

And there were plenty of crises. Indians raided the relay and home stations, looting, burning, and killing. On the trail, the lives of the riders were threatened not only by Indians but by severe weather and natural disasters.

Dangerous as it was, to be a Pony Express rider was a glamorous job. Such legendary western heroes as Wild Bill Hickok and Buffalo Bill Cody rose from the ranks of Pony Express employees. The riders had to be excellent horsemen, young, and lightweight. Because they had to be "willing to risk death daily," orphans were preferred. Yet only one rider lost his life in the service of the Pony. The number of horses who gave their lives to ensure that the mail met its destination has not been counted.

More than a century later, information received quickly is still referred to as being delivered "by Pony Express." The work of the Pony becomes even more impressive when we realize that it rode its way into history in only 18 months.

CHAPTER ONE

⭐

Early Mail Routes

⭐

"The state of California, when she speaks, desires to be heard." —Senator John B. Weller, 1856

The state of California had a problem. Its population had multiplied from 20,000 to 500,000 in little more than five years. Those 500,000 people wanted the same conveniences they had had when they lived in the East. One of these was regular mail service.

People had been moving across the United States to the California Territory in a slow, steady stream. After a war with Mexico in 1848, California became a state in 1850. The new state had every reason to suspect that its population growth would continue at the same slow pace. Then gold was discovered on John Sutter's property in the Sacramento Valley in 1849. Suddenly California was flooded with miners digging for gold in its hills and panning for the precious metal in its streams. Word of a strike would find its way east, sending even more "forty-niners" west to the Golden State to make their fortunes. Ten years after the discovery of gold in California, "Old Pancake" Comstock discovered silver near Pikes Peak in Colorado. Then even more gold was found in Nevada. Stirred by visions of instant wealth, people slapped signs on their wagons reading PIKES PEAK OR BUST, hitched up their mules and horses, and headed west.

Prospectors heading to California, Nevada, or Colorado frequently left their families behind. They intended to send for them once they struck it rich. This could take months, years, or not happen at all. But while these individuals pursued their get-rich-quick schemes, they wanted to be able to get word from home as well as communicate news of their progress in the fields and events in the mining camps to their families back East.

At this time, the railroads did not go any farther west than the Missouri River, so mail could not be transported by train. Without question, the fastest means of communication was the telegraph. But the telegraph lines had not yet conquered the 2,000-mile (3,200-kilometer) span across the North American continent from the frontier town of St. Joseph, Missouri, to the western states that overlooked the Pacific Ocean. How could news and information be safely sent across the country within a reasonable time?

Before the discovery of gold in California, most mail reached the West Coast by ship. Mail and cargo would leave the East Coast, sail south around the tip of South America, and arrive on the West Coast some six months and 13,000 miles (21,000 kilometers) later. Packages were frequently given to an honest-looking passenger, the sender asking the traveler to deliver the parcel to a total stranger. Surprisingly, this system worked fairly well—as long as no one was in a hurry to get the packages and letters at the other end. If the shortcut across the Isthmus of Panama was taken, the trip could be shortened to one month. However, that meant a difficult trek by pack mule and canoe across 50 miles (80 kilometers) of jungle. Then the connection had to be made to the boats on the Pacific side of the isthmus, which ran on an irregular schedule. Ships were also frequently wrecked in storms, their precious cargo sinking with them.

Kansas State Historical Society

Settlers on their way to California during the Gold Rush
pause at a mail station.

When a ship did steam into a California harbor, it caused much excitement. People jammed the docks, anxious for news from the other end of the country. The mail was then delivered to the post office, where eager citizens crowded through the doorways into the building, hoping the bulging mailbags held a letter for them. The postmaster and harried clerks sorted through mountains of mail, trying to place letters into the hands of their intended owners. The process took hours and lines backed up as much as half a mile.

But what about the letters and parcels intended for the miners in the gold and silver fields? It could take weeks to travel from the mines to the nearest town. The prospectors could not risk leaving their claims unattended for that length of time. By the time they returned, someone else might have jumped their claim, and all the work they had done—and possible wealth—would be lost. Still, it was lonely work, and the miners longed for news from family at the eastern end of the country. Several enterprising individuals saw a good business opportunity in filling this need. One of these was Alexander Todd.

An East Coast bookkeeper, Todd caught gold fever in 1849 and headed west. But Todd soon discovered that wading in ice-cold streams and living in mining camps was not for him. He had to make a living somehow, so he hit upon the idea of providing a mail service to the miners in the camps. For $1, a miner could subscribe to Todd's mail service. Todd would then inquire at the San Francisco post office for any mail addressed to the subscribers on his list. If, in fact, there was mail for any of these individuals, Todd would then deliver it to the goldfields for the price of one ounce of gold dust, or about $16 at that time. To have mail carried from the goldfields to San Francisco was much cheaper at $2.50.

The miners were more than willing to pay these rates, and Todd was soon in business as a private mail carrier. He bought two horses, one to ride and the other to carry the mail sacks out of the Sierra foothills. One day, upon arriving in Stockton, some merchants asked Todd to deliver $150,000 in gold dust to San Francisco. Todd agreed, on the condition that they pay him 5 percent of the value of the gold dust. Having no choice, the merchants agreed to the fee. Todd put the valuable material into an old butter keg and boarded a boat for San Francisco $7,500 richer. Almost overnight, he had established himself as an "expressman."

But Todd's express service only operated within the state of California, getting mail to and taking it from the seaport city of San Francisco. Not only did California continue to demand faster east-west and west-east communication, but Colorado and Nevada did as well. This created a need for an overland route. The Oregon Trail, which also became known as the Central Route, was the path used by all the pioneers who had traveled to the Far West. Since it cut through the center of the country, it was the most direct route. Roughly 42,000 people used this trail to cross the plains in 1849 alone.

But the Central Route had its hazards. The stretch between the Mormon capital of Salt Lake City, Utah, west to Placerville, California, was the worst. It was commonly referred to as the "Great American Desert." In the vast territory known as Nevada, there was not one outpost of pioneer civilization. The Indians posed a constant threat to travelers, and the route itself was deceiving. Mountain ridge followed upon mountain ridge, one looking much like the other. It was easy to get lost, and being lost was deadly.

There were miles of dry sagebrush. The ground was infested with alkali, a mineral salt that produced a choking dust when it was stirred up by either horse or wagon wheel. If a traveler survived the desert, the snowcapped Sierra Nevada had to be conquered before reaching California's goldfields.

Still, in an attempt to answer the demand for mail service, the U.S. government contracted with Major George Chorpenning. For a yearly fee of $14,000, Chorpenning, an Indian fighter and trailblazer, was to carry mail from California's capital, Sacramento City, to Salt Lake City and back. The contract was to last three years. Since Chorpenning carried the mail on pack mules, his mail service became known as the "jackass mail."

Chorpenning's service began in May 1851 and functioned well enough until the winter of that year. Once winter set in, Chorpenning's carriers had to deal with severe weather in the Sierras. The path through the mountains was obliterated by heavy snow, forcing the carriers to break trail as they went. The pack animals often froze to death, and the carriers had to continue on foot.

Hostile Indians were also a problem. Chorpenning's business partner, Absalom Woodward, and his entire eastbound mail train disappeared that winter. When their remains were discovered the following spring, it was clear they had been massacred by Indians.

Chorpenning's contract with the government was renewed in 1854. But although he and his staff labored faithfully at their job, their service in the winter months was unreliable. Mail would not arrive at its destination for three or four months. The route through Panama was actually faster. Also, the people in California wanted more than just letters. They wanted newspapers and books. Chorpenning's pack mules could not meet the demands of more weight and less time. Something had to be done.

In the spring of 1856, California senator John B. Weller presented a petition of 75,000 California signatures to Congress. The petition demanded that the U.S. government fund an overland route so that stagecoaches could operate regularly to the distant territory of California.

The U.S. government knew it was in its best interests to keep California's inhabitants happy. Some $300 million worth of gold had already been mined there. Access to that kind of money reserve would come in handy, especially if the trouble brewing between the North and the South continued.

The slavery question had been a powder keg since colonial times, with northern abolitionists squaring off against southern plantation owners over the right to have slaves. The situation had been resolved for a time by the Missouri Compromise of 1820, which stated that for every new slave state admitted to the Union, a new free state had to be admitted as well. While this contained the situation for a time, it did little to ease the tension between North and South. In some ways, it made matters worse. North and South competed to have new states admitted as either free or slave states. And both wanted California's gold.

California was finally admitted as a free state. While this disappointed southerners, it did not stop them from trying to gain a foothold in that state. During the next ten years, southern senators and congressmen and those sympathetic to the South tried to sway California to the southern cause. The South hoped that California would stand with it should a war break out between the states. So, for widely different reasons, both North and South were anxious for rapid and effective communication with California.

On July 1, 1857, the Post Office Department began accepting bids for a new mail route. The next day, pushed by the maneuverings of southern politicians, Postmaster General Aaron Brown announced that he had accepted "bid No. 12,578." The contract was awarded to New York stagecoach operator John Butterfield. But no route was specified in the bid. Instead, it fell to Postmaster Brown to choose the path the mail would follow. Brown, a native Tennessean, chose the southern route.

The North howled. The Chicago *Tribune* called it "one of the greatest swindles ever perpetrated upon the country by the slave holders." New York newspapers nicknamed it "the horseshoe," "the side line," and "the oxbow route." Butterfield, a veteran of transportation, knew the proposed route was 1,000 miles (1,600 kilometers) longer than it should be. He also knew it was open to Indian attack. But the government contract meant a yearly check of $600,000. Butterfield did as he was told.

The "oxbow" actually started in two cities: St. Louis, Missouri, and Memphis, Tennessee. Both routes then met at Fort Smith, Arkansas, and continued west through El Paso, Texas, and on to Fort Yuma on the border between Arizona and California. From there it forked again, one branch going on to San Diego, the other heading north to San Francisco.

Butterfield was to supply service in four-horse coaches seating six passengers and holding three mail sacks and one sack of newspapers. The demands of this contract would have sunk a lesser man of fewer means. But Butterfield put his many resources to work. With the precision of a clock, Butterfield operated a twice-weekly stage along the 2,800-mile (4,500-kilometer) southern loop officially known as the Butterfield Overland Mail Route. On their first run, Butterfield's stages completed their cross-country trek in 23 days and 4 hours. This was 2 days within the 25 days scheduled by the government and caused much excitement at both ends of the country.

Still, by winter of 1859–1860, 23 days was not fast enough. If the abolitionist Abraham Lincoln was elected president, there would most assuredly be civil war. For some time, southern supporters in California had secretly been storing guns and ammunition in preparation for a southern takeover. If California was to be preserved for the Union, it would have to get the news and get it fast.

⭐

CHAPTER TWO

How the Pony Came to Be

⭐

"Have determined to establish a Pony Express . . ."
—William H. Russell

There are several different stories as to how the Pony Express came to be. Some credit the idea to Major Ben Ficklin, trail superintendent for the freighting firm of Russell, Majors, and Waddell. He was assigned to escort California's new senator, William M. Gwin, to Washington, D.C., for his first congressional session. Ficklin knew the way across the country well and felt a regular mail service using overland routes was possible. He suggested the idea to Gwin on their long journey east.

Gwin did introduce a bill to Congress in 1853 that would provide road service between San Francisco and Albuquerque. But there was so much infighting between North and South at this time that little attention was paid to Gwin's suggestion, and the bill failed. Southern senators did not want to lose control of the mail between East and West over the southern route. Northern senators kept lobbying for a move to the Central Route so that they could gain control over the mail service.

In Washington, during the winter of 1859–1860, Senator Gwin chanced to meet William H. Russell at several social functions. It is not clear if Russell, partner in the freighting firm of Russell, Majors, and Waddell, or Gwin brought up the idea of a "horse express." What is known, however, is that Russell left Washington feeling that he had made a commitment to Gwin to start one.

Russell started home. On January 27, 1860, he wired ahead to his son, John, in Lexington, Missouri:

> *Have determined to establish a Pony Express to*
> *Sacramento, California, commencing 3rd April.*
> *Time ten days.*

John, secretary in his father's newly formed Central Overland and Pikes Peak Express Company, understood his father's intention.

He released the telegram to the newspapers.

However, when Russell arrived in the city of Leavenworth in the Kansas Territory, his two partners, Alexander Majors and William Waddell, were less than enthusiastic about Russell's plan. They had formed the Central Overland and Pikes Peak Express Company to pull Russell and another partner out of bankruptcy. In doing so, they had absorbed that company's debts, amounting to $525,532. The firm had also lost approximately $500,000 by freighting supplies and ammunition for the U.S. government during the Mormon War of 1857. Because there had been no time to sign a contract, the firm had simply responded to the government's call. Payment was to come later. But it never did.

Since Senator Gwin could not guarantee a government contract, both Majors and Waddell found the Pony Express idea too risky. Russell, however, saw it as a spectacular way to get themselves out of debt. Such a project would attract worldwide attention, and could shame the government into providing financial assistance somewhere around the $1 million mark. Besides, Russell had promised Gwin in the company's name that they would undertake the venture.

All this sounded a little too familiar to Majors and Waddell. But, being men of their word, they found themselves backed into an honorable—and expensive—corner.

Russell, Majors, and Waddell formed an unlikely trio. Russell was the optimist of the three. He was the company's front man, or salesman, hustling contracts. He had learned frontier merchandising from the ground up during his teenage years when he was employed as a clerk. At the age of 26, he opened a store, Allen, Russell, and Company. Later, he opened another store, Bullard and Russell. This business was successful enough to allow him to purchase property. In 1847, he seized the opportunity to join with another company and send a wagon train to Santa Fe. This venture blossomed into freighting.

William H. Russell

Russell was high-spirited, adventurous, and somewhat reckless. Yet he was one of the most respected businessmen in Missouri. His career had earned him the title of "Napoleon of the West" and afforded him the ability to live in high style. He built a 20-room mansion, complete with a formal garden, stable, and coach house. Dinner at the Russell home was a formal affair. Russell himself always appeared splendidly attired in an elegant black suit.

No one could have been more opposite from William Russell than Alexander Majors. Since his mother's death when he was 6, Majors helped his father with the backbreaking work of building a frontier home in Missouri. He cleared land, split rails, and harvested crops. Majors married when he was 20 and bought his own farm. According to the attitudes of his day, Majors hoped to have several sons who could eventually help him with the work. When his family resulted in five girls, however, Majors decided he had to get into another business in order to raise and educate his daughters properly.

Alexander Majors

Majors started a side business trading with the Indians. He loaded up a wagon with goods he thought would interest the Indians and drove to the Pottawattomi reservation. His trip was so successful that he was able to purchase more wagons. Less than two years later, Majors contracted to haul merchandise to Santa Fe. His business now had 6 wagons and 80 oxen. Majors hired 6 bullwhackers to run the train.

But Majors did not stay at home while his employees worked the trail. Majors was a "man's man," working the routes with his employees. He set strict standards for himself. He read his Bible frequently, never swore, and did not drink. He expected his employees to follow his example and insisted that they take an oath of good conduct upon their employment. This same oath was later taken by Pony Express riders.

Majors developed a reputation for being the best freighter in the West. When he formed the partnership of Russell, Majors, and Waddell, he was the field man, overseeing the actual running of the wagons on the Oregon Trail.

William Waddell handled the money for the business. Like William Russell, Waddell had done service as a clerk. Like Alexander Majors, he had also spent a brief time as a farmer. Unsatisfied with rural life, he opened a dry goods store. That business did well, but Waddell longed to go West. Selling his store, Waddell moved his family to Lexington, Missouri. There he established another store and eventually became one of the major outfitters for those seeking their fortunes in the West in 1849.

Waddell was a member of the same church that William Russell belonged to. The two men became involved in several business ventures together. As the firm of Waddell and Russell, the two contracted to deliver military supplies to Fort Riley in 1853. By January 1, 1855, they signed an agreement with Alexander Majors, forming Russell, Majors, and Waddell. In five years, this would become one of the biggest freighting firms in the country, equal to the Butterfield–Wells Fargo and American Express companies. Majors and Waddell knew that it would be a huge undertaking to launch the Pony Express by Russell's announced April 3 deadline. Despite their misgivings, they nevertheless swung into action.

William B. Waddell

The 1,966 miles (3,164 kilometers) of the Central Route were divided into five divisions. A superintendent was put in charge of each division. All five division superintendents reported directly to Major Ben Ficklin. He, in turn, reported to Russell, Majors, and Waddell. Stagecoach stations already established along the Central Route would double as Pony Express stations. But new stations were needed as well.

Crews were sent out to build the necessary additions. The placement of these stations was determined strictly by the distance the horses could consistently run while maintaining the demanding pace of between 10 and 12 miles (16 and 19 kilometers) per hour. At first, the stations were spaced 25 miles (40 kilometers) apart. Then, when this was considered too difficult, the distance was shortened to 10 to 15 miles (16 to 24 kilometers). Since the success of the Pony Express rested squarely on the backs of its willing and courageous horses, their well-being was of utmost importance.

The stations situated along the route between Sacramento, California, and what is now Carson City, Nevada, were in relatively good locations, allowing for fairly comfortable accommodations for the riders and staff. The same was true of stations at the eastern end between Fort Kearney, Nebraska, and St. Joseph, Missouri. In fact, the riders stationed in St. Joseph were accommodated at the town's luxury hotel, the Patee House. But much of the Pony Express route lay across desert, and there the going was rough.

Supplies were hard to come by in the desert. Water had to be hauled to the stations. Also, since there was no pasture grass for the horses to graze on in these arid regions, hay and feed had to be brought in as well. The feeding of the ponies was critical. Their rations were never shorted. More than once, the grain-fed horses of the Pony Express saved the lives of their riders by being able to outrun the grass-fed ponies of the Indians.

Roads leading to these stations had to be built as well. Before he became a Pony Express rider, Jay G. Kelley assisted division superintendent Bolivar Roberts in building the necessary roads near the Carson River.

> *No amount of money could tempt me to repeat my experience of those days . . . we had to build willow roads, corduroy fashion, across many places along the Carson River, carrying bundles of willows two and three hundred yards in our arms, while the mosquitoes were so thick that it was difficult to tell whether the man was white or black, so thickly were they piled on his neck, face, and arms.*
>
> (As told to Alexander Majors for his book *Seventy Years on the Frontier.*)

After the road was finished, Roberts and his helpers built a relay station out of mud from the lakeshore. To get the mud to the right consistency for building, the men had to trample it with their bare feet. After a week of this, their feet were so swollen from the alkali in the mud that they resembled hams.

Kelley was also responsible for designing a special saddle and saddlebags for the Pony Express riders. Kelley designed a lightweight saddle modeled after the Spanish saddles used by the Mexican *coreos*. He also designed a saddlebag called a *mochila*. The *mochila* fit easily over the saddle. All Pony Express saddles and *mochilas* were made alike so that they were interchangeable. The *mochila* had four pockets called *cantinas:* two positioned in front of the rider's legs and two behind. After the mail was wrapped in oiled silk to protect it from water and sweat, it was locked into these *cantinas*.

Then, of course, horses had to be purchased and the riders hired. An ad appearing in the *Alta California* in March 1860 read:

> *Wanted: Young skinny wiry fellows not over eighteen. Must be expert riders willing to risk death daily. Orphans preferred.*

Hundreds applied. Eighty were chosen.

Russell had given his organization only 65 days to arrange these and many other details. Yet, when April 3 arrived, the Pony Express stood ready to conquer the country on horseback.

CHAPTER THREE

★ Opening Day ★

"Hip, hip, Hurrah for the Pony Carrier!"
—Sacramento *Union,* April 3, 1861

Flags fluttered in the early evening breeze. The city of St. Joseph, Missouri, which claimed to have sent the most settlers west along the Oregon Trail, was about to set another record. But the departure of this single team of horse and rider created more excitement than all the earlier caravans of wagon trains and gold prospectors. For this brave little horse and rider were the key team assigned to start an adventure west across dangerous territory with a deadline that could only be considered superhuman.

Things were not off to a good start. The mail from Washington and New York had left New York three days earlier. But a connection had been missed in Detroit. Word had been telegraphed ahead to the St. Joseph Station that the train was running three hours late.

It was fast approaching five o'clock in the afternoon. The crowd, which had gathered much earlier, was growing restless. St. Joseph's

The Pony Express is born as the first rider leaves St. Joseph, Missouri.

mayor, Jeff Thompson, tried to ease the agitated thousands by instructing the brass band hired specially for the occasion to keep playing. Russell, ever the showman, ordered the little bay mare assigned to make the first run brought from the stable. She was paraded in front of the crowd until people began to pull the hair from her mane and tail for souvenirs. Russell ordered her returned to her stall.

There was some good news from the Hannibal train station, however. Ad Clark was the engineer on the run between Hannibal and

St. Joseph. If anybody could make up lost time, he could. It was on this run, in fact, that Clark set a speed record that was not to be broken for 50 years.

Wells Fargo Bank

The mochila *designed for use by the Pony Express riders*

A special mail car was built for the send-off of the Pony Express. The wood-burning engine, the *Missouri,* chugged out of Hannibal pulling passenger cars as well as the all-important mail car. The train clipped across the tracks spanning the 70 miles (113 kilometers) between Hannibal and Macon at 60 miles (97 kilometers) per hour. The fuel engineer at Macon, knowing that engineer Clark was trying to make time, had a platform built so that wood could be transferred directly onto the train at the height of the engine's storage bins. As the train screeched into Macon, passengers grabbed their seats so that they would not be thrown forward onto the floor. The special platform worked well, as the fuel engineer, stopwatch in hand, counted only 15 seconds that the train was actually stopped to receive the needed fuel.

The *Missouri* sped out of Macon gathering steam for the hilly climb ahead. For the passengers, the rest of this ride was like a roller coaster. Clark charged up the hills at top speed and did not ease up on the downhill runs. When he pulled his train into St. Joseph, Clark had made the 206-mile (332-kilometer) run in 4 hours and 51 minutes. He had made up half an hour.

The Pony Express was now off to a rip-roaring start. The mail the first pony would carry across the country was rushed from the train to the stables. Forty-nine letters, six telegrams, including a congratulatory one from President Buchanan, and special Pony Express editions of newspapers printed on lightweight paper were locked into the *cantinas*. The *mochila* was then slapped onto the saddle of the ever-patient bay mare.

A cannon boomed. The Pony Express was off. The only surviving record of this important day lists William Richardson as the rider astride the bay pony. Picking his way through the throng, Richardson headed toward the Missouri River and the waiting ferryboat, the *Denver.* As Richardson rode his brave mare onto the boat, the crowd across the river at Elwood already roared in welcome.

Once the *Denver* docked, Richardson again had to guide his pony through the crowd of excited Elwood citizens, who also wanted souvenirs from the pony's mane and tail. Since the pony rider's job was to make all speed, these celebrations were not enthusiastically received.

Once clear of these well-intended but hindering folk, Richardson shot forward to the relay stations of Cold Spring, Troy, Lancaster, and Kennekuk. At each of these stations, Richardson changed horses. He then thundered ahead to Granada, where his relief rider, Don Rising, grabbed the *mochila* and continued the mail westward, following the ruts made by the settlers' wagons in the Trail of Scars.

Meanwhile, California, for which this enterprise was begun, was not to be outdone in celebration festivities. Always eager for excitement, the city of San Francisco, though not actually part of the Pony Express route covered by the riders, had prepared quite a show.

The little yellow pony chosen to make the famous first ride east pawed the ground nervously as he was decked out in American flags. Since there had been no time to ship the newly tooled saddles and *mochilas* from one of the three saddleries in Missouri, this first pony sported a western saddle and saddlebags labeled OVERLAND PONY EXPRESS. The crowd in front of the Alta Telegraph office teemed with excitement as James Randall anxiously waited for his mount.

Shortly before four in the afternoon, the pony's saddlebags were stuffed with 85 letters, and Randall prepared to make his first and only ride for the Pony Express.

Since the western end of the Pony Express was actually in Sacramento, Pony Express officials decided it was too costly to send a pony and rider from the Pony Express down to San Francisco only for the purposes of the opening day celebration. Any horse and rider would do. So James Randall and "the little nankeen-colored pony" were pressed into service. Randall proved his lack of horsemanship by mounting his pony from the wrong side.

Nevertheless, they did make an impressive show as they clattered toward the banks of the Sacramento River, where the steamship *Antelope* waited, engines fired, to carry them upriver to Sacramento. For every run

A piece of mail sent by Pony Express

after this historic first one, San Francisco's mail was simply delivered to a waiting steamship, which then carried it upriver to a waiting Pony rider in Sacramento.

Ten hours later, well past two o'clock in the morning, the *Antelope* docked in Sacramento. It had been raining inland for days, and this early morning of April 4 was no exception. There was no send-off for the Pony in Sacramento. The good citizens of California's capital, though no less interested in the success of the venture, had sensibly gone to bed.

Swiftly, the additional mail from Sacramento was added to the saddlebags. It now fell to Sam Hamilton, the key man at the western end of the route, to start the Pony Express on its 2,000-mile (3,200-kilometer) journey.

Hamilton swung into the saddle. No cannon sounded his departure. No crowd cheered. No women waved their handkerchiefs. Without fanfare, Sam Hamilton headed east, splashing through the sleeping city of Sacramento and onto the soggy trail. Into the darkness and the driving rain rode the West's first Pony Express rider.

✪

CHAPTER FOUR

The Route

✪

"Hurrah for the Central Route!"
—Sign in Sacramento store window, 1860.

Hamilton's run was the 45-mile (72-kilometer) stretch between Sacramento and Sportsman's Hall, California. It was too dark to see his pocket watch to check his time. Hamilton had to rely on the rhythm of his pony's hoofbeats pounding along the soggy, flat trail of the Sacramento Valley. Rain in the valley meant snow in the mountains. Hamilton tried to make time so that Warren Upson, the next rider, would have some time to spare when he climbed the white Sierras.

Hamilton sprang from his saddle as he clamored into Five Mile House. He flung the saddlebags onto the saddle of the waiting pony and galloped off. The same routine was repeated at Fifteen Mile House. He was in the foothills now and well on his way to Mormon Tavern.

A rosy glow lit the white caps of the looming Sierras as Hamilton clattered into Placerville. Another fresh horse waited for him; then he was off down the final stretch of his run to Sportsman's Hall. Here, he tossed the saddlebags to his relief rider, Warren Upson. Hamilton had finished his run a half hour ahead of schedule. And Warren Upson needed every extra second as he faced the chilly challenge of the Sierra Nevada.

Warren "Boston" Upson was a daring, gutsy rider. The son of the editor of the Sacramento *Union,* the younger Upson preferred an outdoor life to his father's enclosed one. He learned his riding skills from the Mexican *vaqueros* at some of the biggest *rancherías* in California. A rodeo rider who was equally talented with a gun, Upson had been handpicked to consistently conquer this most rugged and difficult part of the route.

Upson headed for Strawberry Station, named not for the fruit but for the station keeper, who fed straw rather than hay to wagon-train horses but charged hay prices! He crossed the swollen American River, then pressed upward. The trail had become invisible in the snow, which continued to fall heavily. Upson was forced to dismount and break trail for his horse.

Upson walked as much as he rode while the wind funneled through the pass, stinging him with the icy snow. All the familiar landmarks had disappeared in the white blanket. In some places the drifts were twenty feet high. There was always the danger of falling off the trail and into the canyon below.

Changing horses at Hope Valley, Upson pressed on another 21 miles (34 kilometers) to Woodbridge. From there, with the storm behind him, the going was much easier. Upson had still managed a respectable 7 miles (11 kilometers) per hour in the mountains, however. Upson ticked off the miles between Woodbridge and Genoa, then from Genoa to Carson City, Nevada. When he arrived at Friday's Home Station, he had crossed 85 miles (137 kilometers) of rough terrain in unimaginable conditions. It was long after dark when Upson tossed the mail to his relief rider, "Pony" Bob Haslam, and took a much-deserved rest.

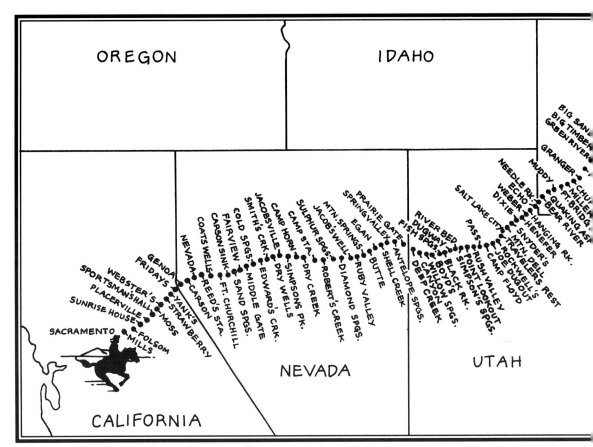

The Pony Express route

As Haslam continued the race east, ahead of him lay a vast desert, stretching across Nevada and part of Utah. Sir Richard F. Burton, an Englishman who traveled the Oregon Trail for adventure, described this part of the route as "a soil alternately sandy and rocky—an iron flat that could not boast of a spear of grass." The Pony riders referred to it as the "most cussed and discussed" stretch of the trail.

The 47 isolated stations sprinkled along the route between eastern Nevada and Salt Lake City offered little more than a fresh horse for the weary rider. Without question, this was the loneliest part of the route. The alkali dust choked both horse and rider as "Pony" Bob thundered across the desert. But Haslam was exposed to more than just the elements on his

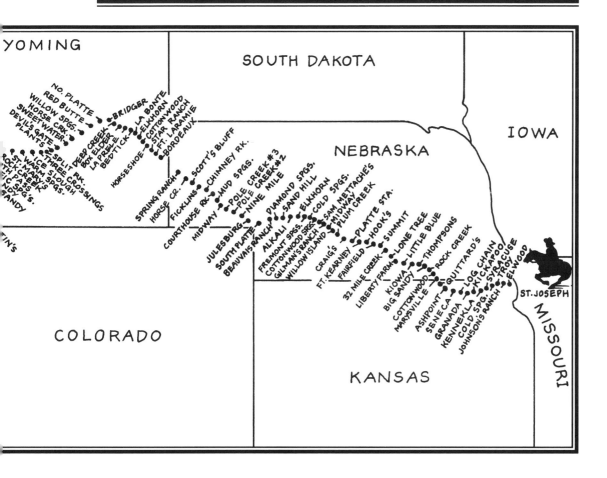

stretch of the run. For this was "Pah-Ute Hell," and while the Indians left the Pony riders alone on the first few runs, they wouldn't for long.

Haslam reached the end of his run at Buckland's Station, where his relief took over. The mail traveled to Ruby Valley on April 6, where William Fisher carried it on to Egan Canyon. William Dennis rushed it to Deep Creek, Utah. At Camp Floyd it was picked up by Howard Egan (after whom Egan Canyon was named), who then ran the mail to the Mormon stronghold of Salt Lake City. Despite weather conditions and hazards, the Pony Express was running 6 hours and 15 minutes ahead of schedule.

As the rider put Salt Lake City behind his pony's hooves, somewhere in the vast expanse of the Utah territory the eastbound rider passed the rider heading west. Though their meeting that Sunday of April 8, 1861, is unrecorded, certainly neither rider paused as much as a second, but thundered past the other in a hurry to recover the other's tracks.

The rider heading east now faced the challenges of the Wyoming wilderness. Early along the trail, the Pony rider paused at Fort Bridger, one of the two military posts located at either end of the state. Then he pressed on through Big Sandy, Little Sandy, and Dry Sandy before reaching the relay station at Pacific Springs. Though this station amounted to nothing more than a crude log cabin with boards placed across boxes for seats, it still provided a fresh mount and rider.

The relief team forged ahead. The rigors of the Continental Divide had yet to be conquered. Pony and rider pressed on past Three Crossings toward the Ice Slough, where, year round, ice remained a few inches below the ground, making tricky footing for the pony. The stark beauty of the Red Desert lay ahead as the rider sped east.

Devil's Gate now loomed ahead. Here the Sweetwater River foamed and cascaded through the 300-foot (91-meter) gorge before the rider could reach the brief relief of Sweetwater Station. An oasis in the desert, Sweetwater Station accommodated both stage drivers and Pony riders. The gentle tinkling of the Sweetwater River was music to the ears of weary and dusty travelers.

Before leaving Wyoming, horse and rider stopped at Fort Laramie, the second Wyoming military outpost, located at the southeast corner of the state. Neither Fort Bridger at the western end of Wyoming nor Fort Laramie in the east functioned as Pony Express stations. Still, the Pony rider faithfully delivered important government documents to the generals from one of the locked saddlebags.

Horse and rider charged ahead toward Chimney Rock, where the towering steeple of that natural landmark pierced the vast blue Nebraska sky. Courthouse Rock and Mud Springs lay ahead, then Old Julesburg. It was at Julesburg that one of two events occurred that almost brought the first run of the Pony Express to a sudden halt.

Now swollen by spring rains, the Platte River ran just outside of Julesburg. As horse and rider attempted to cross it, the river swept the horse off its feet and carried it swiftly downstream toward quicksand. Fortunately, a crowd had gathered on the opposite side of the riverbank to cheer the rider on. The rider grabbed the saddlebags and splashed ashore. One of the spectators volunteered his horse to the Pony rider. The rider accepted and left his own horse to be rescued by the crowd.

The other near-disaster happened to the rider heading west. Things had gone well for Thomas Owen King for the first 20 miles (32 kilometers) out of Fort Bridger. Five miles (8 kilometers) later, however, he ran into a storm. The trail was narrow and the ground uneven. King's horse stumbled, throwing him and his precious cargo to the ground. The wind blew the *mochila* over a cliff. King managed to recover it and continued on, arriving at Echo Canyon on schedule.

Another third of the trail remained to the east of Julesburg. There was a sign at O'Fallon's trading post that informed the rider that he was now 400 miles (644 kilometers) from St. Joseph. Horse and rider raced to Cottonwood Springs. Also known as McDonald's Ranch, it doubled as a home station for the Pony Express as well as a station for the Overland stage.

The mailbag flew through the air once again, landing on the saddle of a fresh horse. Continuing east, horse and rider passed through Midway, another home station, given its name because it was located midway between Atchison and Denver, Colorado. After Plum Creek, the Pony Express paused once again for the military at Fort Kearney.

From Fort Kearney, Nebraska, to the end of the line in St. Joseph, conditions on the trail began to improve. When the rider reached Rock Creek Station at the eastern end of Nebraska, he was coming down the home stretch. Adventurer Sir Richard F. Burton described the remainder of the route east as "deep, tangled wood, elms, hickory, basswood, black walnut, poplar, hackberry, box elder and willow, bound and festooned by wild moss and creepers, and an under growth of white alder and red sumac." After the barren Red Desert, all this greenery must have been a relief to both pony and rider.

At the home station of Seneca, Kansas, a fresh horse and rider continued the journey east through Log Chain, Kickapoo, and Kennykirk. Boarding the ferry at Elwood, the Pony rider then thundered into St. Joseph, Missouri, at 5:00 P.M. on April 13, 1860. The first run of 1,966 miles (3,164 kilometers) had been made in the scheduled ten days.

A tumultuous welcome awaited horse and rider. Fireworks lit the sky, bonfires blazed, and the cannon that had announced the rider's departure ten days earlier now boomed in praise of a job well done.

Meanwhile, at the western end of the route, the good citizens of Sacramento realized that they had made no preparations to receive the newfound hero. On the morning of April 13, when the Sacramento *Union* suggested that horse and rider be received with all due honors, the town became a hub of activity. Nobody knew exactly when they would arrive, but they knew it would be late that afternoon. Women leaned over balcony rails while men and boys climbed roofs, poles, and anything that would give them a bird's-eye view of the approaching rider.

At 5:25 in the afternoon a cloud of dust was spotted on the Fort Sutter road. "Here he comes!" someone shouted, and California's capital became hysterical with excitement. Here, too, cannons boomed and guns were fired. A welcoming committee lined the road to greet Sam Hamilton. As he approached, they whirled their horses around and spurred them back toward Sacramento, leaving Hamilton and his tired pony choking on their dust.

A puzzled and somewhat irritated Hamilton rode into town. No one had seen him off in the early hours of the miserable morning of April 4. Why had all these people turned out now? After all, they were slowing him down.

Disgruntled, Hamilton rode to the Pony Express office, where Sacramento's mail was sorted out. The *mochila* was returned to Hamilton, who remounted his pony and headed for the steamship *Antelope,* which

California State Library

*The first westbound rider, Sam Hamilton, arrives at the end
of his route to a torchlit parade.*

was waiting to carry the two to San Francisco. When they docked around
12:30 in the morning of April 14, fire rockets, courtesy of the Monumental
Fire Engine Company, streaked across the sky while bells rang. More cannons were fired and the California Band burst into "See, the Conquering
Hero Comes."

The weary Hamilton now faced a celebration bigger than the one
that had taken him by surprise in Sacramento. For San Francisco had
organized a parade in honor of the Pony Express, and Hamilton and his
pony were the main attraction. The parade did, however, lead Hamilton
to his final destination, the Alta Telegraph Office. Here he was finally able
to unburden himself of the *mochila*. He had done his job. Thanks to its
horses and riders, the Pony Express had come through.

CHAPTER FIVE

★

Riders and Famous Rides

★

". . . and the swift phantom of the desert was gone."
—Mark Twain, *Roughing It*

hen the word went out that the freighting firm of Russell, Majors, and Waddell was looking for express riders, hundreds of young men applied. The high salary of $25 a week was undoubtedly a lure. But so was the promise of adventure. Only 80 applicants fit the specific requirements, however.

First, Alexander Majors insisted that the riders be of high moral character. Each rider had to take an oath before he could be hired:

I do hereby swear before the great and living God that during my engagement, and while I am an employee of Russell, Majors and Waddell, I will under no circumstances use profane language; that I will drink no intoxicating liquors; that I will not quarrel or fight with other employees of the firm, and that in every respect, I will conduct myself honestly, be faithful to my duties and so direct all my acts as to win the confidence of my employers. So help me God.

Majors also insisted that every animal be treated well. Nothing would bring dismissal as fast as an act of cruelty to any animal in the care of the firm: horse, oxen, or any other.

After completing the oath, each rider was given two revolvers, a Spencer carbine shotgun, and a Bible. The riders considered the shotgun too heavy and cumbersome, however, and did not carry it for long. The same can be said of the Bible. There simply was no place to put it on either horse or rider. Despite their oath, it is also difficult to imagine these riders not uttering some colorful language when they were being hotly pursued by Indians.

The riders were also given horns to sound their arrival as they approached a station. Both riders and stationmasters quickly realized that the horn was unnecessary, however. The sound of the hoofbeats or a cloud of dust was enough warning for the station attendants. The riders also adopted a "coyote yell" to alert the station as they drew near.

When things were running normally, the stationmasters could rely on the punctuality of the riders to determine their arrival times. So did ordinary citizens, who actually set their watches by the passing of a Pony rider, dependable clocks being hard to find on the frontier.

In the beginning, the Pony riders had a kind of uniform: red shirts, slouch hats, and denim jeans from Levi Strauss tucked into boots. This uniform was quickly abandoned, however, and the riders wore whatever was most comfortable to them.

To ride the pint-sized, powerhouse ponies, the riders had to be pint-sized powerhouses themselves. They could not weigh more than 120 pounds (54 kilograms). To maintain the average speed of 10 to 12 miles (16 to 19 kilometers) per hour in the saddle, they had to be skilled horsemen able to ride anything, anytime, anywhere.

Each rider was assigned a specific run. They would change horses every 10 to 15 miles (16 to 24 kilometers), allowing only two minutes for the switch. Frequently, this change of mounts was accomplished in 15 seconds and the rider was off on his next stretch. When a rider's path crossed over mountains, his run averaged 55 miles (89 kilometers) in length. The flat runs through the desert and plains averaged 120 miles (193 kilometers), as they were considered not as difficult—until the trouble began with the Indians.

The job of a Pony Express rider was not for the timid. This was a difficult and dangerous job. The demands on both horse and rider were rigorous. If a rider was not being chased by Indians, he was fending off horse thieves anxious to steal the excellent animals of the Pony Express. It was these adventures that made some of the Pony riders legendary. One of the most famous was young William F. Cody, better known in later years as Buffalo Bill.

When Cody's father died, young Bill went to work for the freighting firm of Russell, Majors, and Waddell. He was only 12 years old, but he felt he had to support his mother and his sisters. He was hired as a messenger, assigned to ride between wagon trains on the road to Utah. In the evenings, when the wagons had set up camp for the night, he practiced learning how to write by scratching letters into the wagon wheels. But, having an adventurous spirit—a major requirement for a Pony rider—Cody begged to be allowed to ride for the Pony Express.

While there are those who question whether Cody actually rode for the Pony Express, it seems that Alexander Majors, who had a fondness for the boy, eventually gave in and gave Cody a short 45-mile (72-kilometer) run in Jack Slade's division. Slade was less than enthusiastic about having this "kid" in his charge. However, when he saw how well

Cody could ride, he transferred the youngster to the 116-mile (187-kilometer) stretch between Red Buttes and Three Crossings, one of the most dangerous of the entire route.

Like "Pony" Bob Haslam, Cody rode more than just his route when the situation called for it. In fact, Cody holds the record for the longest nonstop ride in Pony Express history. Galloping into Three Crossings one day, he learned that his relief rider had been killed the night before in a drunken brawl. (So much for the oath.) Without hesitation, Cody grabbed a fresh horse and rode on, adding 76 miles (122 kilometers) to his scheduled run. When he reached Rocky Ridge, he immediately turned back east toward his home station. When he arrived safely at Red Buttes, he had covered 384 miles (618 kilometers), leaving the saddle only long enough to change horses.

Along with being a good rider, Cody also proved quick-witted in dangerous situations. On a day off, Cody, now 15, was out hunting sage hens in the brush near his station. As he was cooking the birds, he was surprised by outlaws who demanded his horse. Cody obliged them and started to lead them to his animal, which was tied nearby. But young Bill had a trick up his sleeve. He took one of the hens with him as he walked to his horse. When he pretended to drop it, one of the rustlers stooped to pick it up. Cody cracked the thief over the head with the butt of his revolver, shot the other bandit, jumped onto his horse, and escaped.

Bill Cody was the youngest of the Pony riders. At first, the Pony Express did not want anyone under the age of 18. That rule was overlooked in Cody's case and the cases of several of his companions in the saddle.

William F. Cody at age 14

St. Joseph Museum

The average age of the riders was 22. Yet, in spite of their young age, there was a high turnover rate in riders. Of the first 80 riders hired, few remained after the first year. The summer months weren't too bad, but the riders dropped out regularly during the winter of 1860–1861. Some lasted for several weeks, some for several days. Very few remained Pony riders the entire 18 months of its existence. Some of them joined the army of either the Union or the Confederacy when the Civil War broke out in April 1861. For most, however, the physical strain was simply too much. Many were the times that station attendants and stock tenders were pressed into immediate service when a Pony rider simply could not go on.

This was the case of James Butler Hickok, who later achieved fame as "Wild Bill." At the age of 24, he was employed by Russell, Majors, and Waddell as a stock tender. Though he is not officially listed as a Pony rider, he undoubtedly jumped into the saddle and covered for some of the riders when the situation demanded it.

So exhausting was the job that more than one rider fell asleep in the saddle. Nineteen-year-old Jack Keetley rode into Seneca sound asleep after doubling for another rider, logging 340 miles (547 kilometers) in 31 hours. Another rider, Thomas Owen King, recalled in later years that he fell asleep in the saddle many times.

> *I remember once I came into Bear River after a night ride of eighty miles from Salt Lake, and reported to the station keeper that I had not passed Henry Worley, who was riding in the opposite direction. Worley had reported the same thing about me at the other station. We had both been so sound asleep in our saddles that we did not know when we passed each other. The ponies, when they learned what was expected of them, would keep up the pace from one end of the run to the other.*

Because their job was so dangerous, Pony riders were much admired. They created quite a stir whenever they rode by. Writer Mark Twain hoped to see a Pony rider when he traveled to Nevada. Riding in a Concord coach he described as a "cradle on wheels" (though the drivers cursed the Concord as a "Pitching Betsy"), Twain's wish was granted.

> *Every neck is stretched further and every eye strained wider. Away across the endless dead level of the prairie a black speck appears against the sky . . . . In a second or two it becomes a horse and rider, rising and falling, rising and falling . . . nearer and nearer still, and the flutter of the hoofs comes faintly to the ear—another instant and a whoop and hurrah from our upper deck, a wave of the rider's hand . . . and man and horse . . . go swinging away like the belated fragment of a storm.*

Johnnie Frye, a rider between St. Joseph and Seneca, was the object of affection of many young women who lived in the towns along his route. They would wait for Frye with cakes and cookies, passing them to him as he rode by. But they noticed he had trouble holding on to the cookies with his one free hand, the other holding the reins. So these clever young ladies came up with the idea of making the cookies with a hole in the center. That way Frye could stick his fingers through them and collect them more easily.

But Frye's gift givers were also interested in souvenirs. One young woman wanted to sew Frye's red necktie into her "log cabin" quilt. Frye, however, would not part with his trademark. So the determined young woman saddled a horse and waited for Frye to ride by on his scheduled run. As Frye approached, the young seamstress kept pace alongside his horse and asked again to have the tie. Frye still refused and, in a playful spirit, put spurs to his horse. Not to be outdone, the young woman charged after him. As she caught up with him, she reached for the red tie.

She missed, but was able to grab hold of Frye's shirttail, which she tore loose. She returned happily home with her trophy and sewed the piece of shirttail into the quilt.

So admired were the Pony riders that regular citizens were eager to assist whenever they could. One day the rider on the run from Folsom to Sacramento fell from his horse and broke his leg. Luckily, a Wells Fargo stage happened by. One of its passengers, J. G. McCall, volunteered to finish the run for the injured rider. McCall was greeted by a cheering crowd when he arrived in Sacramento.

In early March 1861, riders were asked to push themselves and their ponies even harder. Then Abraham Lincoln, the abolitionist lawyer from Illinois, was elected president and took office on March 4. With the ever-increasing tension between North and South, the citizens in the far-flung frontier were eager to learn what President Lincoln had to say. Lincoln's inaugural address was telegraphed from Washington to St. Joseph and from St. Joseph to Fort Kearney. From there, it was raced by Pony riders across the frigid, snowy mountains and plains. It was very rough going. Several horses lost their lives in the attempt.

Still, the Pony Express set a record: 7 days and 17 hours to Sacramento, where the message was telegraphed to San Francisco.

The speed of the Pony riders impressed everyone who saw them flash by—including the Indians. Howard Ransom "Ras" Egan volunteered to replace a rider too sick to ride out of Shell Creek Station. Toward dark, he saw the glow of a campfire up ahead in Egan Canyon. Egan rightly assumed the fire meant Indians. He also figured that if there was one group of Indians in the canyon, another group must be close by.

Egan took out his revolver, put spurs to his horse, and charged the Indian camp, yelling for all he was worth. The startled Indians scattered, figuring that there must be a large party of white men nearby. Egan reached his last station safely. Later he learned that the Indians had set a trap for the Pony riders through Egan Canyon. They wanted to find out what the riders carried that made them go so fast.

CHAPTER SIX

The Ponies

". . . the veritable Hippogriff who shoved a continent behind his hoofs so easily."
—San Francisco *Bulletin,* April 14, 1860

Although the riders received the attention, the unsung heroes of this adventure are the ponies. Nothing could have been accomplished without these brave little horses. Frequently, they saved the lives of their riders by their endurance, speed, and heart. Many gave their lives in the service of this venture to which they lent their name.

As early as February 10, 1860, the Leavenworth *Daily Times* advertised for "200 grey mares." Actually, between 400 and 500 horses were needed. It is doubtful that those purchasing the horses cared what color or sex they were. What mattered was whether or not they could do the job.

As grueling as the job was for the riders, it was more so for the ponies. They had to maintain an average speed of 12 miles (19 kilometers) per hour over distances of 10 to 15 miles (16 to 24 kilometers). This pace and distance is difficult for a horse to maintain under the best circumstances. The conditions of the Pony Express were rarely good. For this reason, only the best horses would do.

Horses were purchased both privately and at auction. The going rate for a horse at this time was $50. The Central Overland and Pikes Peak Express Company paid from $150 to $200 for a good horse.

At the eastern end of the Pony Express route, the horses purchased were mostly "blooded" horses, or Thoroughbreds. A good number of them came from the bluegrass state of Kentucky, known for producing high-quality racing Thoroughbreds. As speed was a primary consideration in the operation of the Pony Express, buying racing stock made sense.

A Thoroughbred is a specific breed of horse, its name meaning "bred through" and referring to the purity of its blood, or heritage. The Thoroughbred originated in England and was developed by crossing a domestic English country horse with the exotic and fleet Godolphin Arabian. The cross produced a streamlined, lanky horse with speed and endurance. As a breed, the Thoroughbred was scarcely a century old at the time the Pony Express went scouting for suitable animals. But its qualifications for the job were obvious, the flat plains of Kansas and Nebraska being like one long racetrack.

The horses were called ponies because of their height. By definition, a pony cannot be over 14 hands, 2 inches high. (A *hand* is a measurement of 4 inches, the term coming from the method used to measure a horse's height before the invention of the measuring stick. The hand is held sideways and the horse is measured from the ground to its withers, the high point on its back where the base of its neck joins its spine.) The weight of these animals averaged 900 pounds (405 kilograms).

Height and weight were specific requirements for Pony Express horses. Big horses could not perform the job. Their bodies were too stout

Midway Pony Express Station located on Lower "96" Ranch in Nebraska

and their legs too long, particularly for the mountainous regions of the West. So the western end of the Pony Express rounded up mustangs.

The mustang is a descendant of the Spanish horses brought to Mexico by Hernando Cortés. Flimsy corrals allowed the horses to escape. Some wandered off while grazing, and some were stolen by Indians. Some horses moved farther south into Mexico. Others migrated north to what would become the American West. On their way, they were joined by other horses that had strayed from the Spanish missions, and by lost Indian ponies. The result of the interbreeding of these wild horses resulted in the *mestengo,* or mustang. These tough little horses roamed free on the ranges and were known for their intelligence, hardiness, and speed.

The beginning of the Pony Express could not have been better as far as acquiring mustangs was concerned. The best time to capture these horses is in the early spring. They become colicky on the rich new grass and, due to the intestinal discomfort, are not able to run as fast. It is easy to then round them up with horses fed on hay and grain. To this day, they are still captured in the same way.

All the horses were rushed into service for the Pony Express, leaving little or no time for training. What schooling they had was done by either the station keeper or one of the attendants. They were the only ones who had the time—when they weren't fighting Indians or fending off marauders. "Training" usually amounted to getting a saddle on the horse's back, a bridle over its head, and a bit in its mouth. Peter Neece, station keeper at Willow Creek, considered a horse trained "when a rider could lead it out of the stable without getting his head kicked off."

For many of these horses, the first time they were ridden was when a Pony Express rider mounted and rode them out on a scheduled run. Naturally, the horses would buck. As a result, the first few minutes of the ride were more like a rodeo than a mail relay.

Years in the wild made the mustang an independent creature. Accepting the rider's tack, or equipment, was bad enough. But then this feisty animal was asked to accept steel shoes on its hardy hooves. It could take as many as three men to shoe a mustang. First, the horse had to be thrown to the ground. Then, with one man sitting on the horse's head and another sitting on its hindquarters, the farrier would attempt to trim and shoe the flailing hooves. This was a procedure that could take up the better part of a day.

But it was this determination of spirit that made the mustang the choice of several Pony Express riders. These durable ponies could be depended on to climb the Sierra Nevada, survive the desert, and cross the Continental Divide. Hardy as they were, however, they were still flesh and blood, bone and sinew. Many horses broke down on the trail, leaving their riders to continue sadly on without them, on foot. The West, indeed the United States, owes these animals a great debt.

CHAPTER SEVEN

★

Stations

★

"There were only four men at each station and the Indians . . . roamed over the country in bands of thirty to a hundred."

—Colonel Hungerford, U.S. Cavalry

As many adventures as the Pony Express riders had while on the trail, those who remained at the stations did not lack for excitement. The jobs of the stationmasters and attendants demanded the utmost in loyalty and dedication. Without them, the Pony Express could not function. Yet, in many cases, the men who ran the stations were sitting ducks for any number of catastrophes— and they knew it.

This was lonely territory for the station attendants, with only the howling of the wolves and the yipping of the coyotes to keep them company. The relay stations, in particular, were almost impossible to defend. Built of whatever materials were handy, many of these so-called stations were crude constructions of adobe mud. Some were nothing more than rough shacks or tents. If building supplies were not readily available, the station was simply dug out of the side of a hill.

The relay, or swing, stations housed one station keeper and a stock tender. It was their job to look after three or four horses kept in corrals only a few feet from the station itself. Most of the stations had dirt floors, and the furniture consisted of whatever crates or boxes the residents could press into service. For beds, the men either slept inside on the floor or outside on hay or straw or in a wagon box.

The bigger home stations marked the beginning or ending of a rider's route. Usually they were old stagecoach stations and were better equipped. The home stations housed the station keeper, two to four stock tenders, two riders, several horses, and other animals, as well as extra equipment. Here, the beds were pole bunks built into the wall.

The food was coarse at all the stations. Some of the stations hired professional hunters to bring in fresh meat, but the staples were usually dried meat, beans, dried fruit, and coffee. Bread was baked fresh at the station. Water was obtained from a nearby source such as a lake, pond, or stream and was frequently of questionable quality.

The five divisions of the Pony Express route were run by the division superintendents. It was the superintendent's job to maintain the stretch of trail assigned to him. As a result, division superintendents spent most of their time riding their stretch of the route.

Their duties also included seeing that the stations were supplied and that the livestock were well kept. They hired or found replacement riders when those scheduled to ride either became sick or suddenly quit. They also had to fight off Indian attacks, cattle rustlers, and horse thieves. In the more western regions of the route, the Pony Express division superintendent was the only recognizable form of law within his district. For this reason, only men of high moral standards were chosen. One of the best—and worst—division superintendents was Jack Slade.

Slade was in charge of the line between Old Julesburg, Colorado, and South Pass City, Wyoming. Julesburg was named for its stationmaster, Jules Reni, a French trapper and Indian trader. Located far from anything remotely resembling civilization, Julesburg was little more than a collection of tumbledown shacks that had never seen a paintbrush. Its name struck fear into the hearts of travelers.

Located at the junction of the Pikes Peak Road and the Overland Trail, Julesburg was home base for a crowd of outlaws and thieves. When the Central Overland and Pikes Peak Express Company took over the Central Route, Julesburg had to be cleaned out. A man rougher than the ruffians was needed. Jack Slade was just the man for the job.

Slade's reputation preceded him. He had killed his first man when he was 13. Exiled to Texas, his experiences in the war with Mexico had seasoned him. He was a hard-drinking man, known for his skill with a revolver. Slade knew that Julesburg was a haven for frontier outlaws and figured Jules Reni was the leader of the pack. The first thing he did was dismiss Reni from his position of stationmaster.

Reni was furious. He ambushed Slade and pumped him full of buckshot from a double-barreled shotgun. Slade, however, survived, had the buckshot removed in St. Louis, and returned to get his revenge on Reni.

He found Reni at Pacific Springs. Reni tried to escape on horseback, but Slade knocked him from his saddle with a bullet to his hip. He then lashed the injured man to a corral post and, between shots of whiskey, used Reni for target practice. Reni died, peppered by 22 bullet holes. Slade then cut off the dead man's ears, carrying one around in his pocket as a souvenir.

It would appear that in the effort to clean out Julesburg, Slade's moral character was overlooked. However, his work for his employers was always excellent. When sober, he was courteous and efficient. Mark Twain, who met Slade at a station west of Julesburg, described Slade as "the most gentlemanly, quiet and affable officer on the Overland service." His division had the reputation for being the best run on the route.

It was his activities outside the job that were questionable. Slade was eventually dismissed after one too many drunken sprees. According

St. Joseph Museum

Cottonwood Station in Hanover, Kansas

to "Pony" Bob Haslam, Slade got his comeuppance in Montana, where he was hanged for wrecking one too many saloons.

Some of the stations along the nearly 2,000 miles (3,200 kilometers) of the Pony Express route had the same name. There were two Cottonwood Stations, for example. There were also two stations named Rock Creek. It was at the Rock Creek Station in Nebraska that the famous shootout took place between David McCanles and Wild Bill Hickok.

In the spring of 1861, one year after the Pony Express began its operations, James Butler Hickok, an employee of Russell, Majors, and Waddell, was sent to Rock Creek Station to recover from a near-fatal scrap with a bear. While he was on the mend, he was put in charge of the livestock.

Rock Creek Station was owned by David McCanles, who rented the property to Russell, Majors, and Waddell. When the 23-year-old Hickok arrived at Rock Creek, McCanles took an instant disliking to him. He made quite a show of knocking the injured and therefore defenseless Hickok to the ground. McCanles assigned Hickok to a crude dugout by what is now known as Wild Bill's Creek.

When McCanles finished making improvements to his property, he sold it to the Overland Stage Company. They, in turn, established their own man, Horace Wellman, as Rock Creek superintendent. The Overland Stage Company made arrangements to pay McCanles in monthly installments. However, due to the strapped financial conditions of the company at this time, the June payment was missed, then the one due in July. McCanles was irritated and hounded stationmaster Wellman daily for the money. Wellman, being an employee of the company and not in charge of finances, was powerless to help McCanles and told him as much.

This angered McCanles even further. On the afternoon of July 12, McCanles loaded his gun and rode to Rock Creek, spoiling for a fight. Accompanying him were his cousin, James Woods, his 12-year-old son, Monroe, and one of his employees, James Gordon. With this kind of backup, it was obvious McCanles planned to make good his threat to "clean up on the folks at the ranch."

As they rode to the Rock Creek ranch house, McCanles instructed Woods and Gordon to wait, out of sight, at the barn. If they heard anything that sounded like trouble, they were to come to his aid immediately. He and his son then rode to the house and dismounted, leaving their horses at the well.

McCanles was met at the side door by Wellman. McCanles launched into a tirade, threatening to repossess the property by force if the money was not paid immediately. Wellman repeated what he had told McCanles time and time again. Even though the company had not given Wellman the money to pay McCanles, he was not authorized to give up the property. When McCanles became even angrier, Wellman left the doorway.

Then Wellman's wife came to the door. She had had several earlier run-ins with McCanles herself and was ready to give him a piece of her mind. She was interrupted by Hickok.

The unexpected appearance of his enemy at the ranch house flustered McCanles. When Bill Hickok was angry, his eyes stared cold and blank. That look meant big trouble. McCanles settled down a bit and asked to speak to Wellman again. Hickok went back into the house.

McCanles then went around to the front door of the house, where he had a clear view inside and a clean line of fire. As an excuse, McCanles asked for some water. Hickok handed him a dipper, then walked behind a calico curtain that divided the house into sleeping quarters and living area. McCanles, aware of the danger in which he had placed himself, called to Hickok to come out and fight. When Hickok did not appear, McCanles started into the house. His advance was arrested by a shot through his heart. McCanles fell back into the yard and into the arms of his son. He died almost instantly.

Meanwhile, Gordon and Woods, having heard the shot, came running around the side of the barn. Woods ran toward the kitchen, where he was dealt two shots from Hickok's revolver, smoking behind the kitchen door. Woods staggered around the side of the house, where he collapsed in a clump of weeds.

Gordon reached the front door in time to see Hickok shoot Woods. In a panic, he ran back to the barn, hoping to escape on his horse. Hickok fired twice. Wounded, Gordon turned and ran through the brush down to the creek bed. Hickok chased him, shooting until he had emptied both his revolvers.

Hickok raced back to the house to reload his weapons. There he came upon the gruesome sight of the crazed Mrs. Wellman finishing off Woods with a hoe. Intending to repeat her performance, she headed for the McCanles boy, who was still bending over the dead body of his father.

Horrified, Hickok wrested the bloody weapon from her, and Monroe was able to escape.

A bloodhound was now set on Gordon's trail through the brush along the creek. When the dog found him, Gordon was shot and buried where he stood. His body was cast into a shallow grave, his boots still on.

Hickok was arrested for murder three days later. The charges were dismissed, however, on the grounds that he was defending government property used to carry the U.S. mail.

Not every dispute at the stations was settled with a gun, however. Early in 1861, a stage driver nicknamed Rowdy Pete arrived at Green River Station sporting a small U.S. flag. But the sympathies of the station keeper lay with the southern Confederacy. The station keeper told Rowdy Pete never to display the flag again. But the next time Rowdy Pete pulled his coach into Green River Station, he had it decorated down to the wheels with American flags.

CHAPTER EIGHT

Indian War

*"We will burn the stations . . . and we will kill the
pony men."* —Gosiute Indian, 1860

The Pony Express had made only
eight trips across the country when it began having trouble with Indians.
The winter of 1860 had been unusually harsh and the medicine men of the
Pah-Ute tribe blamed the white men for their problems. To the Indians,
the immigrants were "bad medicine." The Pah-Utes, particularly the
younger members of the tribe, were ready for war.

The Indians met at Pyramid Lake to decide what should be done
about the white invaders. The Pah-Ute chief, Numaga, fasted for three
days, hoping to urge his tribe toward a peaceful settlement. However,
while the elders of the tribe were discussing the problem, some of the
younger members stole away from the conference and, on May 7, raided
Williams' Station. Five men were killed, the station was burned, and the
war was on. During the next two months, other Pony Express stations

were raided, horses and livestock were driven off, and more men were killed. Other tribes joined the Pah-Utes. By June, the Sioux, the Cheyenne, the Shoshone, and the Arapaho lurked along 250 miles (400 kilometers) of the Pony Express route. The life of every Pony rider was in danger every time he put his left foot in the stirrup.

The Indian uprising led to some adventurous times not only for the riders but for those at the stations as well. William Streeper, a carrier of heavy mail, loaded his pack mules one June morning and set off on his normal delivery route. He knew there were Indians about but decided to brave the situation. When he arrived at Simpson's Park, he found the stock gone, the station burned, and the station keeper dead. Streeper hurried on to Smith's Creek, where he spent the night, little realizing that the worst was yet to come.

The following morning, Streeper headed east on his return trip, accompanied by two gold prospectors heading toward Salt Lake City. There was no sign of life when they reached Dry Creek Station other than a herd of cattle moving away from the station. After the previous day's experience, Streeper moved cautiously to the door. In front of him lay the hair-raising sight of the scalped and mutilated body of stationmaster Ralph Rosier. The body of station attendant John Applegate lay nearby. The other station attendant, Lafayette Bolwinkle, had managed to make a run for it to the next station. When the Indians attacked the station, "Bolly" had bolted from bed in his stockinged feet. He made the 10-mile (16-kilometer) run to the nearest station without benefit of boots. When he arrived, his feet were swollen, filled with cactus needles, and so badly cut by stones that he was unable to walk for some time.

Rider Nick Wilson also had several run-ins with Indians. Riding his normal route, Wilson arrived at Deep Creek Station to discover no relief rider waiting for him. Wilson rode on to Willow Creek, where station-master Peter Neece told him his relief rider at Deep Creek had been killed. Wilson passed the *mochila* to another rider and stayed at Willow Creek.

Seven Indians rode up to the station and demanded food. It was not uncommon for stationmasters to give some supplies to Indians to keep things friendly. Neece gave them a 20-pound (44-kilogram) sack of flour. The Indians demanded a sack for each of them. Neece became angry and gave them nothing. The Indians showed their displeasure by shooting an arrow into an old lame cow in a nearby pen. Neece was furious at this display of cruelty and shot two of the Indians. The remaining five ran.

Neece knew there were some 30 Indians camped nearby. He and the other three men at the station loaded every gun they had and prepared for an attack. Just before dark, a cloud of dust announced the arrival of the Indians. One of the men started to sob in fear.

Neece moved his men outside into the brush, telling them to stay down and apart. When the Indians arrived, they were confused by gunfire coming from outside the station. Whenever Neece and his men fired, they would jump to another spot to avoid being shot by return fire. Finally the Indians gave up and rode away.

Another of Wilson's adventures with the Indians scarred him for life. One evening, as he was having dinner at Antelope Station, he and the stock tenders noticed the horses being run off by Indians. The men started after them. The Indians ran into a nearby cedar grove. Wilson chased after them and was struck in the head by an Indian arrow. The arrow lodged in Wilson's forehead, two inches above his left eye. Wilson's two companions tried to remove the arrow, but the shaft broke, leaving the point in his head. Leaving him for dead, the two men rolled Wilson under a tree and ran for the next station.

The next morning, they returned to the cedar grove to bury Wilson. Much to their surprise, he was still alive. They carried Wilson to Cedar Wells and sent for the nearest doctor, who was a day's ride away. The doctor removed the arrow from Wilson's head but gave him little chance to live. He told Wilson's companions to keep a wet rag on his head, and left. Six days later, division superintendent Major Howard Egan

An artist's representation of an Indian raid on a Pony Express rider

was passing through and, seeing Wilson hovering between life and death, sent for the doctor again. The doctor redoubled his efforts, and Wilson lay unconscious for 12 more days. Wilson finally did recover. However, the arrowhead left such a noticeable scar on his forehead that he would never take his hat off, not even at mealtimes.

It was during the Indian war that "Pony" Bob Haslam made his famous ride from his home station near Lake Tahoe to Carson Sink and back. Not long after that record 380-mile (612-kilometer) ride, he ran into 30 armed Pah-Utes blocking the trail. Haslam took out his revolver and rode, full speed, at the Indians. The leader of the group, impressed by Bob's daring, shouted "You pretty good fellow" and signaled the others to let "Pony" Bob pass. Not a shot was fired.

Long before William F. Cody became known as Buffalo Bill, he was a rider for the Pony Express. While riding out of Horse Creek one day, the 15-year-old Cody was chased by Indians. He managed to escape them by lying flat on his pony's neck and digging in his spurs. Cody owed his young life to the swift, well-fed pony who outdistanced the Indian horses.

Yet despite these and many other similar incidents, only one rider was killed during the Indian war. One day, a Mexican youth, José Zowgaltz, rode into Dry Creek Station slumped over his saddle horn. The *mochila,* soaked in blood, continued west with the relief rider. But the injured Zowgaltz went no farther. Despite the best efforts of the station attendants, his wound was fatal and he died within a few hours of his arrival.

One of the most dramatic episodes occurred at Egan's Station. It was early in the morning and stationmaster Mike Holt and one of the Pony riders were having breakfast. Suddenly they were surrounded by a large number of Indians. Grabbing their guns, the two men defended the station until their ammunition ran out. The Indians broke through the door and their leader spoke one word, "bread." He ordered the two men to build a fire and bake fresh bread. This they did all day, the Indians devouring it as fast as it came out of the oven. Around sundown, Holt ran out of flour. The chief then ordered the two white men taken outside, where they were tied to a wagon tongue driven into the ground. Dry sagebrush was piled around them and lit. The Indians danced around the two men in eager anticipation of seeing them roasted alive.

Just then, from over the hill came Pony Express rider William Dennis. With him was the U.S. Cavalry, flags flying and bugles blowing. Dennis had approached the station earlier on his scheduled run. However, seeing the Indians from a distance, he had spun his horse around and raced back five miles, where he had passed Lieutenant Weed and his unit on their way to Salt Lake City. Dennis knew that Indians at the station spelled trouble. He and the cavalry arrived just in time to save the two men from being burned at the stake.

The Indian war caused the Pony Express to cease operating for one month. Public demand forced the government to send in the army to end the uprising. In fact, Lieutenant Weed's timely arrival at Egan's Station seems to have dealt the final blow to the Indian resistance. Eighteen Indians were killed and 60 horses captured. The Indians quieted down after that defeat.

Still, the losses for the Pony Express were great. Sixteen men were killed, 150 horses driven off, and seven stations burned. By the time the costs of rebuilding the stations and getting new stock were figured into the loss column, Russell, Majors, and Waddell had lost $75,000 in the Indian war. This was not good news to a firm that could ill afford to lose a single cent.

★

CHAPTER NINE

The End of the Line

★

"Goodbye, Pony" —California *Pacific,* October 1861

Russell bargained on the Pony Express being a spectacular achievement, and it was. So widespread was the Pony's fame that it captured the imaginations of people as far away as England, France, and Germany. Artists for British and French newspapers and magazines were quick to draw their impressions of what a Pony rider looked like as he raced the mail across the country. The British were so taken by the Pony Express that the London *Illustrated News* sent a reporter to the United States to see the Pony in action.

Europeans also used the services of the Pony Express. The end of the 19th century marked the beginning of European investment in the American West. European businesses with offices on the West Coast were delighted with the swift services of the Pony Express. Those who had invested in the western mining operations of Nevada, Colorado, and California found the speedy communication with their field representatives invaluable.

The British also used the Pony Express to communicate with their holdings in the Far East. The information traveled by ship from England to New York, was then telegraphed from New York to St. Joseph, raced to Sacramento by Pony Express, was telegraphed to San Francisco, then again traveled by ship to the Orient. As complicated as this process may sound, it worked well and effectively sped up communication.

But for all the admiration it received, the Pony Express could not pay its bills. Right from the beginning, Alexander Majors and William Waddell knew the venture was too risky without the guarantee of a government contract. At $5 an ounce, the cost of the Pony service was expensive. It was not used casually. But even if more people had used its services, the Pony would not have met its expenses. At $25,000 a month, the cost of running the operation far exceeded what it was able to earn. The losses resulting from the Indian war didn't help, either.

In November 1860, Russell lobbied hard in Washington, trying to get the much-needed mail contract. By now the Pony Express had proven as reliable a service across the Central Route as Butterfield's mail service was across the southern. But the political climate in Washington was electric in agitated anticipation of the Civil War. Without realizing it, Russell became a pawn on the chessboard of a southern plot.

In an attempt to raise funds for his failing firm, Russell spoke with Secretary of War John B. Floyd. Russell was honest. He told Floyd just how desperate his company's financial situation had become. Floyd suggested that Russell talk to Godard Bailey, custodian of the Indian Trust Fund. On two separate occasions, Bailey arranged for Russell to have Indian bonds that Russell could then use to obtain short-term loans and keep his business going.

Then, on December 24, 1860, the newspapers released information of the loss of $3 million worth of Indian bonds. Though only $387,000 was

Rock Creek Station, Nebraska

attributed to Russell, the truth was that Bailey had no authority to give Russell the bonds. They belonged to the Indians. In short, Bailey's releasing of the bonds—and Russell's acceptance of them—was illegal.

Russell was immediately arrested in his New York office. Bailey had conveniently disappeared, but was arrested later. When the details of the scandal were sorted out, they revealed a Confederate conspiracy. Pressure had been mounting between North and South as the South continually threatened to leave the Union. Bailey and Secretary of War Floyd, both southern sympathizers, had attempted to drain the U.S. government of its cash reserves. It would be difficult for the North to challenge southern secession if the Union had no money to finance a war.

Yet, during all of this turmoil, the horses of the Pony Express continued to run. Somehow, the salaries and needs of the Pony Express were met. This put a strain on the other operations of the Central Overland

and Pikes Peak Express Company. Payroll for the freighting operation fell so far behind that its employees nicknamed the company "Clean Out of Cash and Poor Pay."

Russell was released on bail shortly after his arrest. Both he and Bailey were indicted by a grand jury in Washington on January 30, 1861. Floyd had escaped to the southern state of Virginia at the first hint of trouble.

By February 1861, the U.S. government knew that civil war was unavoidable. John Butterfield was ordered to move his mail-carrying service from the southern to the Central Route. Russell had no choice but to merge the Pony Express with the Butterfield–Wells Fargo Company. It then became known as the Overland Mail Company and ran the route west from Salt Lake City to Sacramento. The route east from Salt Lake City was taken over by Benjamin Holladay, one of Russell, Majors, and Waddell's biggest creditors.

In March of the same year, the government granted a $1 million contract to the Butterfield–Wells Fargo Company. The contract specified a six-day-a-week stage service and the continuation of the Pony Express "until the completion of the transcontinental telegraph."

At long last, the U.S. government had acknowledged the Pony Express. But it was too little, too late. Russell's board of directors demanded his resignation in April and Russell's brilliant business career was over. The "Napoleon of the West" had fallen from his throne.

The Pony Express had always been thought of as a temporary solution to the problem of cross-country communication. It was obvious that the telegraph would eventually span the width of the North American continent. In fact, two months after the Pony Express had begun operating, Congress passed an act guaranteeing a yearly sum of $40,000 for ten years to any company that could connect the existing telegraph lines from east to west. No one stepped forward right away, however, because of the Indians. After all, the new telegraph wires would run right through the heart of Indian hunting and burial grounds.

But the Civil War broke out in April 1861, creating a bigger need for even faster communication. Edward Creighton, a young telegraph contractor, now traveled the Pony Express route to investigate the building of telegraph wires.

The Indians had quieted down after their defeat in the Indian war ten months earlier. But Creighton wanted to make sure he had no trouble with them. He knew the Indians were superstitious, and he used this to his advantage. As the line was built, Creighton invited two Indian chiefs to "talk" with each other, one being positioned at Fort Bridger and the other at Horseshoe Station. The Shoshone chief asked a question. The message was wired to the Sioux chief, who answered back. Several questions and answers were then wired back and forth. Puzzled, the two Indian chiefs agreed to meet face-to-face and compare notes. When they did, they were convinced that the "talking wires" were the work of spirits.

The telegraph construction crews also used Indian labor to assist them in building the lines. One day, a thunderstorm broke out over a valley of the Sierra Nevada, charging the telegraph wires with electricity. When the storm had passed, the men went back to work tightening the wire. Knowing the danger, the white workmen wore heavy leather gloves to protect themselves. The Indians, however, grabbed hold of the wire with their bare hands. The wires held just enough electricity to knock them flat. The Indians ran in fear, and the word spread among the tribes that the "talking wires" were "bad medicine."

Work on the transcontinental telegraph began in July 1861. As the construction crews labored to extend the lines, the gap between the telegraph terminals began to close. For the Pony riders, this meant they had less and less distance to travel. On October 24, the first transcontinental telegram was wired from San Francisco to Washington, D.C., and the services of the Pony Express were no longer needed. The Pony came to an official end two days later.

Despite the benefit the telegraph provided of seemingly instant communication, the country mourned for the Pony. It had lost a trusted and much-loved friend. A writer for the Sacramento *Daily Bee* wrote:

> *Nothing that has flesh and blood and sinews was able to overtake your energy . . . but a senseless, soulless thing that eats not, sleeps not, tires not . . . has encompassed, overthrown and routed you. This is no disgrace, for flesh and blood cannot always war against the elements.*

A writer for the California *Pacific* echoed these thoughts in his article:

> *A fast and faithful friend has the Pony been to our far off state. Summer and winter, storm and shine, day and night, he has traveled like a weaver's shuttle back and forth til now his work is done. Goodbye, Pony! . . . You have served us well.*

AFTERWORD

"But ghostly riders flit on ghostly mounts
And skim the twilit ways with silent feet."
—Charles Joseph Carey, "Pony Express Courier"

In a way, the Pony Express could be thought of as the first Wild West Show. In fact, in later years, after little Bill Cody had grown up to become Buffalo Bill, his touring show would not have been complete without the exciting reenactments of Pony riders and their adventures.

What became of those daring young men in the saddle? Some, like Cody, had as much or more success in later careers. When the Pony Express closed shop, Cody worked as a scout. Later, he was hired by the railroads to hunt buffalo for its construction crews. It was in this job that he earned the nickname he would later make famous. "Buffalo Bill's Wild West Show" was a success not only in the United States, but in Europe as well.

Joining Cody briefly on stage was Wild Bill Hickok. Frequently described as the physical model of manhood, Hickok did not take naturally to showmanship, and returned to life in the West. For a man so admired by others, he met with a brutal end. Tragically, he was shot in the back of the head at point-blank range while playing cards in a saloon. He died instantly.

*A Pony Express rider salutes the arrival of the telegraph,
which would eventually make the Pony Express obsolete.*

Johnnie Frye, whose shirttail was sewn into a quilt, enlisted in the Union army shortly after the Civil War began. He was killed by Confederate soldiers.

"Pony" Bob Haslam rode for Wells Fargo, served as a deputy marshal, then, in later years, worked for one of the big hotels in Chicago. He carried a business card that had a sketch of him on horseback, making his famous ride through "Pah-Ute Hell" in the spring of 1860. He died at the age of 72.

Sam Gilson discovered the mineral Uintahite in the Utah mines. The mineral had an asphalt base and Gilson discovered it was good for building roads. The mineral was renamed Gilsonite in his honor, and he became very wealthy as a result of his discovery.

Russell, Majors, and Waddell did not fare so well. Russell's reputation was ruined by the bond scandal. He was shunned by those who used to dote on him. Eventually his health failed, and he died at the home of his son, John, at the age of 60.

Alexander Majors continued in freighting for a while, then tried his hand at mining in Utah. This failed, however. He was reduced to poverty in his later years, and Bill Cody found him living in a shack in Denver, writing his memoirs. Now world famous, Cody had always been grateful for the kindness Majors had shown him and his family. He hired an editor to supervise the writing of the book. Cody then paid to have it published under the title *Seventy Years on the Frontier.*

The remainder of William Waddell's life was as tragic as those of his two partners. He did not attempt any more business ventures, but remained in his home in Lexington, Missouri. During the Civil War, his home was raided repeatedly. Later, some of his property was sold for back taxes. He died at the age of 65 in the home of his daughter.

Senator Gwin, who liked to be thought of as the godfather of the Pony Express, never did lift a finger to help it. At the outbreak of the Civil War, Gwin, whose term expired in 1861, toured the world extensively. Eventually he established himself in Mexico as colonization adviser to ruler Maximilian, who gave him the title "Duke of Sonora." After the fall of Maximilian's government, Gwin ended up in San Francisco in poverty.

In these days of overnight mail and communication by phone and fax machine, it may be hard to understand how an entire country could get so excited about horses running back and forth from one end of it to the other. But the Pony Express is western adventure at its best. Despite the fact that it was a financial failure, its dedication to its work and its triumph over impossible odds became the symbol of a growing America. The adventures its riders had on the trail inspired the imaginations of people all over the country—indeed, all over the world. Its job completed after only 18 months, the passing of the Pony marked the end of an era.

But even today, there are places in Wyoming and the Great American Desert where the Oregon Trail is much the same as it was when the ponies' hooves pounded over it more than a century ago. Listen carefully, for the hoofbeats of the Pony Express echo through time.

Further Reading

Ahlborn, Richard E. *Man Made Mobile.* Washington, D.C.: Smithsonian Institution Press, 1980.

Blackman, Henry, Weybright Blackman, and Victoria Sell. *Buffalo Bill and the Wild West.* New York: Oxford University Press, 1955.

Bradley, Glenn D. *The Story of the Pony Express.* Chicago: A. C. McClurg, 1923.

The Bureau of Land Management. *Competing with Time.* Washington D.C.: Bureau of Land Management, 1976.

Chapman, Arthur. *The Pony Express.* New York: Putnam, 1932.

Connelly, William E. *Wild Bill and His Era.* Press of the Pioneers, 1933.

Day, David. *Entrepreneurs of the Old West.* New York: Knopf, 1986.

Hafen, Le Roy. *The Overland Mail.* Cleveland, Ohio: Arthur H. Clark, 1926.

Harlow, Alvin F. *Old Post Bags.* New York: D. Appleton, 1928.

Hoffman, H. William. *Sagas of Old Western Travel and Transport.* San Diego: Howell N. Books, 1980.

Howard, Robert West. *Hoofbeats of Destiny.* New York: New American Library, 1960.

Mattes, Merrill J., and Paul Henderson. *The Pony Express, From St. Joseph to Fort Laramie.* Lincoln, Nebr.: Patrice Press, 1989.

Morton, J. Sterling. *Illustrated History of Nebraska* (Third Volume). Lincoln, Nebr.: Lincoln Western, 1911.

Nevin, David. *The Expressmen.* New York: Time-Life Books, 1974.

Nottage, James H. and Jim Wilke. *Stagecoach! The Romantic Western Vehicle.* (Museum Study Series, Vol. 1, No. 1) Los Angeles: Gene Autry Western Heritage Museum, 1990.

Settle, Raymond W. and Mary Lund. *Saddles and Spurs.* Lincoln, Nebr.: University of Nebraska Press, 1955.

Visscher, William Lightfoot. *A Thrilling and Truthful History of the Pony Express.* Skokie, Ill.: Rand McNally, 1908.

Wilson, Neil C. *Treasure Express.* New York: Macmillan, 1936.

Index